W 12/05 W 8/09 W 3/13 W 1/15

Candle Time

Kwanzaa

Denise M. Jordan

Heinemann Library
Chicago, Illinois

© 2002 Reed Educational & Professional Publishing
Published by Heinemann Library,
an imprint of Reed Educational & Professional Publishing,
Chicago, Illinois

Customer Service 888-454-2279
Visit our website at www.heinemannlibrary.com

Designed by Sue Emerson, Heinemann Library; Page layout by Ginkgo Creative, Inc.
Printed and bound in the U.S.A by Lake Book

06 05 04 03 02
10 9 8 7 6 5 4 3 2 1

Library of Congress Cataloging-in-Publication Data
Jordan, Denise M.
  Kwanzaa / Denise Jordan.
    p. cm. — (Candle time)
Includes index.
Summary: A brief introduction to the celebration of Kwanzaa.
  ISBN 1-58810-528-8 (HC), ISBN 1-58810-737-X (Pbk.)
  1. Kwanzaa—Juvenile literature. [1. Kwanzaa. 2. Holidays. 3. African
  Americans—Social life and customs.] I. Title. II. Series.
  GT4403.A2 J67 2002
  394.261—dc21
                            2001004631

Acknowledgments
The author and publishers are grateful to the following for permission to reproduce copyright material:
pp. 4, 5, 8, 9, 11, 12, 14, 15, 17, 20, 21, 22 Lawrence Migdale; pp. 7, 10 Jake Wyman; p. 13 Esbin /Anderson/ Omni-Photo Communications; p. 16 Maril Delly/Ethnographics; p. 18 Craig Mitchelldyer; p. 19 Cathy Melloan

Cover photograph courtesy of Maril Delly/Ethnographics

Every effort has been made to contact copyright holders of any material reproduced in this book.
Any omissions will be rectified in subsequent printings if notice is given to the publisher.

Special thanks to our advisory panel for their help in the preparation of this book:
Eileen Day, Preschool Teacher
Chicago, IL

Paula Fischer, K–1 Teacher
Indianapolis, IN

Sandra Gilbert,
Library Media Specialist
Houston, TX

Angela Leeper,
Educational Consultant
North Carolina Department
of Public Instruction
Raleigh, NC

Pam McDonald, Reading Teacher
Winter Springs, FL

Melinda Murphy,
Library Media Specialist
Houston, TX

Helen Rosenberg, MLS
Chicago, IL

Anna Marie Varakin,
Reading Instructor
Western Maryland College

Some words are shown in bold, **like this.**
You can find them in the picture glossary on page 23.

Contents

What Is Kwanzaa?

Kwanzaa is a candle time.

It is an African-American holiday.

Kwanzaa celebrates African Americans working together.

It is a time to show older people that they are special.

When Do People Celebrate Kwanzaa?

DECEMBER						
1	2	3	4	5	6	7
8	9	10	11	12	13	14
15	16	17	18	19	20	21
22	23	24	25	26	27	28
29	30	31	1			

Kwanzaa begins on December 26.

Kwanzaa lasts for seven days.

What Do People Do During Kwanzaa?

Family and friends tell stories about the past.

They sing, play games, and dance.

People show things they have made.

Sometimes, children put on a play.

What Lights Are There During Kwanzaa?

kinara

People put candles in a candleholder called a **kinara**.

The candles are red, black, and green.

They light a different candle
every day.

What Do Kwanzaa Decorations Look Like?

bendera

Some people hang up an African-American flag.

It is called a **bendera**.

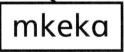

| unity cup | mkeka |

They put fruit, ears of corn, and a **unity cup** on a **mkeka**.

The unity cup is a sign of togetherness.

What Foods Do People Eat During Kwanzaa?

Some people eat corn, chicken, and **collard greens.**

Other people eat African foods like peanut pudding.

unity cup

The food goes on the **mkeka**.

Everyone sips juice from the
unity cup.

How Do People Dress for Kwanzaa?

dashiki

Kwanzaa is a good time to wear African clothing.

Men and boys may wear long, loose shirts called **dashikis**.

Women and girls may wear dresses made from **kente cloth.**

What Games Do People Play During Kwanzaa?

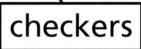
checkers

Kwanzaa is a time for families to play together.

Some families play **checkers**.

Others play African counting games like **mancala**.

Are There Gifts for Kwanzaa?

Kwanzaa presents are called **zawadi**.

This girl is making Kwanzaa gifts.

Many Kwanzaa gifts are homemade.

People get gifts for doing something special.

Quiz

Here are some things you see during Kwanzaa.

Can you name them?

Look for the answers on page 24.

?   ?   ?   ?

Picture Glossary

bendera
(ben-DARE-ah)
page 12

checkers
page 18

collard greens
page 14

dashiki
(dah-SHE-kee)
page 16

kente cloth
(KEN-tay kloth)
page 17

kinara
(kee-NAH-rah)
page 10

mancala
(man-KAH-lah)
page 19

mkeka
(m-KAY-cah)
pages 13, 15

unity cup
page 13, 15

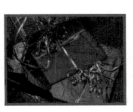
zawadi
(zah-WAH-dee)
page 20

23

Note to Parents and Teachers

Reading for information is an important part of a child's literacy development. Learning begins with a question about something. Help children think of themselves as investigators and researchers by encouraging their questions about the world around them. Each chapter in this book begins with a question. Read the question together. Look at the pictures. Talk about what you think the answer might be. Then read the text to find out if your predictions were correct. Think of other questions you could ask about the topic, and discuss where you might find the answers. Assist children in using the picture glossary and the index to practice new vocabulary and research skills.

Index

Answers to quiz on page 22

mkeka | kinara | unity cup | dashiki